Idiom of the American Boy

Rick Duffey

For Lynne Marie

Cover design: The Erie Street Press Studio
Graphic Illustration of RickDuffey by Eric Duffey

ISBN 979-8-218-74125-9

Idiom of the American Boy

INDEX

METAPHYSICS OF BLACK STARS

Tonight the ordinary sky
looks more like a redacted document
or maybe it's the mood I'm in
which is not so much
a mood as the absence of a mood
a mitten instead of a glove
tonight the universe is opaque
like one of those black stars
those stars undreamed of
before the Hubble
look   all day I haul around inside
my own body waiting for
unanswered phone calls
watching feeble TV   & all day
it's like there's a rat caught in
my trousers trying to escape
& all this night I contemplate
the metaphysics of black stars
which makes me the gatekeeper
to absolute nowhere
nobody wants in nobody wants out
tonight my pockets are filled
with receipts
I've no idea why I saved them all

WILLIE THE GRAY PUDDING WHO KILLS FOR PLEASURE

i

willie who is huge & gray
willie who is patient like the reaper
who waits beside the glue boards
for the occasional sacrificial rodent
willie who prefers to sleep
on sour old oriental carpets
willie the gray pudding who kills
for pleasure who stares at the space
between bookcase & floor
where perhaps some
careless ultrasonic squeak
confirms the condition of
original sin the occasion of
conditional sin

ii

m'self I sit in my decrepit recliner
I watch my cat hunting mice those
toga-like corpses of flickering bone
willie knows nothing of this of course
but strives to extinguish
one heart at a time
one heart no bigger than a match-head
no thicker than a scream

iii

I am still asleep willie is awake
wandering the whole upstairs
looking for something to kill
willie silent as a lynx
enters my kill-zone
perhaps there is a mouse I wake

iv

I sweat like a too-ripe melon & see
 this gray blob

something throbbing in his jaws
slip out into the hallway
like a neutral fog
hungry for meat

                    v
willie returns from his midnight shift
up from the basement with empty teeth
nights of pink mouthfuls behind him
willie jumps up into my lap
perhaps there's a wounded mouse
inside my pants
somewhere between the stucco
the red sea parts

KARAOKE NIGHT AT THE OK CORRAL

Then I drank a jeroboam

Then I drank a rehoboam

Then I drank a pint of Sav-Way Scotch

Then I threw it up

All of it I threw it up hurled it up a notch

Then I limped to London

Then I crawled to France

Then I slept on ceilings & watched the mattress dance

& Then I got religion

Then I read a book

Then I dug night-crawlers   impaled them on a hook

Then my applications were rejected

Then my motives were suspected

& then I lost religion & could no longer function

Then I went out seeking Extreme Unction

Then I took up politics   politics & epidermis

A crown of thorns   a penis

Then I met Arithmetic somewhere near Damascus

Then I studied further   then I earned my masters

Then I climbed a mountain of happily ever afters

Then fell off a mountain   the same damn mountain

Landed in the fountain

Then I fell through ice

Then I met a wife

Then I turned quite empty in a carnival of plenty

Then I crashed Oktoberfest in Marti Gras attire

Then I flayed my ego   impaled it on a wire

Then I smoked a green cigar

Then I smoked a black cigar for quick relief

Then I smacked an angel in her perfect angel teeth

Then I made Confession

Then I crossed an ocean

Then I blamed The Virgin

blamed it on emotion

& then I lost my will

& then I wandered like a stone

A stone with sticky feet

& then I drank a jeroboam

& then I drank a rehoboam

then I drank a pint of Sav-Way Scotch

DRESSER OF SYCAMORES

I don't believe in unicorns   I don't
I believe in rain
I don't believe in heroes or unhappy endings
I don't believe in the failure of hammers
or the forfeits of old wine
but I do believe in rain

You may believe in the Jehovah of capital improvement
go right ahead   Congratulations
If you ferment in your own ambrosia
in the newfangled zeitgeist of melted wax   in the hordes
& multitudes made into spent cartridges   continue as you will
it's your faux baptism but as for me having been here before
& before that I still believe in rain

You only believe in those prophets with honey
with flannel by Jesus   Body By Flasher
thick sweet words to live by like with like
& as with as   but as for me I continue to hang
with harsh sackcloth shepherds & I don't
believe in the perfectibility of men I don't believe
in the cleansing properties of woman's fire
no I do not
but I do believe in rain

PARKING LOT THUGS IN DANGER OF ACCIDENTAL BUDDHAHOOD

                              for bill rust & greg oliva

our bodies glow under
he mercury vapor like those
radioactive statues of the sacred heart
they used to sell to catholic school children & fuses
dangle on our lips like cigarettes

we are the local high profile losers
still hanging   we will do just fine whatever
they send to us earthquakes
or volcanoes prophets or pestilence we will
never be undersold   but till that happens we
grow absurdly gentle in our python-skin
sneakers faint as cheap tattoos which
you can't tell anymore are they eagles
or roses clenched between the mandibles

our numbers decline by marriage by prison
or premature death or simple maturation
yet we lean backwards avoiding
the sidewalk's grid & taking no prisoners
except to freak out cotton-headed
christian ladies on their way
to wednesday night bible study
at the second pentecostal because
their devil's much harder than ours

even the beer we drink passes
right through us without losing color
just foam just bubbles.

50th YEAR CLASS REUNION

Pushing sixty & nine & looking
Like hell on a slab of toast
Vandalized by gravity

(Reminds one of eulogy)

Faces all stuffed with creases
Neck tendons & lariats
Jocks who never made TV

Or the potlatch Olympics

& plus of course naturally
The pom-pom squad gone to fat
They gather in the ball room

Of a local country club
Like old operation scars
All over a stretched abdomen

Youthful appendectomies
Writ large late in middle age

Some never even made it
Their urns on mantelpieces
Forwarding their best regards

Their plots of newly sodded
Rectangles   Eternity
Making former classmates sad

But wine & frivolity

In front of all the cameras
The blood-letting must go on
All in spite of the Reaper
Or because of the Reaper

& you can stand on the stump
& you can count all the rings

Tell the wet years from the dry
Calculate all the seasons
By fossilized cadmium

Go get drunk on the golf course
Vomit champagne Armpits full
& make love to the new moon
That dark spot where no stars spawn

You'd think that Gray's elegy
Fast forwarded to our time
Might make for a fine blueprint

Except we lack the dignity
Cheap shoes with expensive soles
Remembering only memory
Statutory innocence

A SORT OF TESTAMENT

If I must come back at all let me return
as a life
form that does not shit
that has no sense of smell
that does not fall in love like falling off a shark's nose
that cannot fail but to breathe in smoke under

Let me return like a shoe without weather
like an adlib   "row row row your boat"

I mean if I must come back at all
like reflux of sunshine & shadow
allow me to expand like a monkey's fist
shaking the doors to his trap or
Let me return   if I have to return
like a springtime rain or a summer thunderstorm
or that kind of autumn drenching that rips away
the remaining leaves   or a
winter rain colder than real snow   Just not
a rainbow or concerto or something anything
stuck inside a scented envelope.

If I'm not yet done   like a Buddhist Catholic
trapped between the two views of it
let me be reborn with bones
inside my tongue & fingers pointing out
into the profound unknown.

Unless I'm simply dispersed in
the manner of an unscented aerosol
let me return as a sort of perhaps
a parasitic wheel   rimless   exposed
& laughing like a planet.

A VISITOR FROM 2019

I can tell by the coldness in your voice
18 hours up from arkansas
thermos coffee overdose that
you are wired too tired
for immediate sleep that my lights
inside are too harsh for
your night eyes so we sit awhile
on the front steps
& kill off the last of ezra
brooks I make you take the
rest
of the meatloaf a few stale buttermilk
biscuits & some peaches from the tree
out back I finally got around
to spraying this spring
I know that you'll wake recharged
mid afternoon to find yourself
some urgent business down the road
saving me the embarrassment of
telling you circumstances
that you can not stay here
& I palm you that twenty which you've
the good charity to take muttering
something that half a truth
that I still owe you from that incident
seven years ago   goodbye
we make the grim farewell at the gray
unpainted fence your face
like raw boot-leather my face pink
with burning & peeling
I note the condition of your fenders
bubbled & rusted like my gutters
still clogged with last year's leaves
you hope to make des moines
by midnight you with your eight
perfect women all awaiting

the ultimate in human sacrifice
& me stuck on the pavement
like an uncanceled stamp
I hear myself saying how
I envy you your liberty
johnny fucking appleseed
you calling me
your rock of gibraltar

BOBBY'S WAKE

my dead buddy sure looks good dead but good his
mama made them cut his hair & beard & plaster or
glue

him back together put him in a 3 piece

suit borrowed from from the closet from a dead uncle
elegant also recently buried also 40 regular red tie with
blue sailboats such as a grandpa might wear

to a tuba recital my dead buddy looks less

like a failed troubadour than perhaps a failed shoe
salesman you'd never guess how he made
his living suffering bad piano

in an elegant airport lounge which catered

to transient adulterers cashing in Bach & Chopin
to put his wife through graduate school

me I shake with his surviving male relatives

surviving uncles who smell like Aqua Velva in
mothballs as for me I tell his mama how sorry how
it's such a waste & she tells me through clenched
teeth it is all part of god's plan & we both focus our
eyes at the floor I mean who the hell wants to be
part of god's plan here in this elegant gilt foyer

full of green velveteen folding chairs
& artificial braided ficus

& so I continue my condolences working those
edges of the room where seated almost forgotten I
n deep vermilion is my dead buddy's great
grandmother who is only 1 percent still alive

older than the last surviving confederate widow &
I step outside for a sec only to breathe in new air
not recently exhaled by mourners standing in
clumps to pay respects to somebody my dead
buddy somebody they all have written off any
way & I meet his wife my dead buddy's still warm

elegant wife sucking down her Virginia Slims her
eyes sugary from all the pills they've been
feeding her every 4 hours & she hugs me though
it's well known she doesn't like me very much
she says "I shouldn't be here now should I

it's finals I should be home cramming but I guess
if I don't know it all by now I never will!"

At 18th & MICHIGAN

brown weeds
white rubbish

urban decay like rotten food
themes of experience

here pedestrians
step quick time

here the walls close inward

the rhinoceros-hided sidewalks
turn into suspicious rubble
nothing to mention except

the occasional sad graffiti

across the vacant southwest
corner you can see

where some squatters
have made a home by joining two
defunct Chevies with a striped
bedspread not too far

from the beautiful steeple

of a now defunct Presbyterian
congregation

all this waiting for the issues
of guns & turf to be settled

so that rehabbers from the Northside
can live in fortress lofts where
Capone's beer once flowed
like sow's milk above
these same sidewalks
I would not come here at all but
for inertia & obligations but for
neglect & bad decisions

BREATHING DOUBLE LIVES (a thought experiment)

Today I am the gravedigger out of
    hamlet & I'm Feste the clown
    out of uniform
    some window opens to admit
    the owl of responsibility

the basement rises up to swallow

    leftover panther   the
    remnants of uneaten panther

some feral pig delicious in its intentions
    moves like a hungry glacier

    a dead mattress implodes behind
    my mirror shades   & I
    wake with "Hey Joe" singing in
    my ears I fake public kindness

    & I devour bread

people don' think I bite but I bite

    deep inside there's a viper about
    the length of a school day an echo
    which loses what it ought repeat

    hello becomes hell   hell
    becomes heh & leaves me stranded
    there

    like a discarded tube
    or a can of ether

& meanwhile I attempt my best impression
    of the human male in his own

personal skin part bear & half
buffalo

I go through today with a bucket
        and sponge trying to look useful
        but what the bear desires

    the buffalo despises

DEAD TOMATOES

bless her my mama
she could not tolerate
        dead tomatoes
fists of scarlet edible nightshade
garden vines listing sideways
stems & leaves
like crumpled brown seaweed
a thousand miles inland
she hated death my mama
maybe the war maybe the depression
maybe those visits
to the vast necropolises halfway
out long island
where they had to bury the Catholics
two or three coffins deep
whatever nothing
should linger after the last harvest
my mama hated dead tomatoes
or even the rumor
of dead tomatoes
come the first prediction of killer frost
then back into the house they fled
green as green grapes green
as old timothy hay these last
of the season swaddled or shrouded
in newsprint on the sill to ripen
as best they can & to taste
like the rotten vinegar memories
of good meat
my mama how she hated dead tomatoes
but now that I'm old
enough to feel ill-used when a cold wind
unwinds at me
I see my mama's point
it's like the claw of a hammer
& not just any hammer

October's bitter hammer
I would like thank you mama for giving me
fair warning
this death inside   it's coming

DRINKING SCHLITZ & SMOKING CAMELS

Meanwhile across town
Mara prepares to sing
"Red River Valley"
but she shudders instead
as someone walks over her grave.
That someone is me
of course, trimming hedges
at Fairview Memorial park.
The hearse driver,
who is also Mara's
ex fiancee twice removed,
provides useful toothpicks
to all who still have teeth.
He waves buckets at me. It's a tough funeral
overall with all those
black-shirted pall bearers
drinking Schlitz & smoking Camels.
Beware of drinking dirt lager.
Mara, take care not to go
sticking your tongue down my throat!
I have complicated responses. Any day now
you can expect
to hear my scream. I can feel something
with eight tiny legs
creeping up my neck.

MY CHEAP MOTEL

How cheap was my motel?
      Bullet holes in the plaster
      A resident's plaster disaster

The hallway carpet stinking of piss
Beside the ice machine   this

Always out of order
Inject another quarter?
INJECT A DISK O BLISS?
      Entire place just inches short of hell
      Weekend rates
just ring that bell
How cheap indeed was my motel?

I wake up Claudia, tell her that it's snowing,
Suggest we go dancing as naked as the moon
Such WAXING overflowing, turning blue too soon
Outside the trees beyond the parking lot
Beyond the vapor lamps and outta sight
She raises one & tells me go to hell
      So tell
Me right away How cheap was my motel
How cheap   (excuse me bargain rates
     Off-season rates)   how cheap
was it my motel?
With a disinfectant stench your mama's corpse could smell
The lobby furniture cozy as the morgue
A dot com feel   maybe a dot org
You book your rooms on line   what line?
Smells like vintage muscatel   How cheap
O Lord was my motel

Cheap by two inches cheap the bulletproof divide
     Was my motel   the zombie clerk jerk
Who looked a lot like old Dubuque

Who reading yesterday's USA Today
Does not look up   not right away
"You want a room?   You got the means to pay?"
          how cheap Cheap CHEAP was my motel?
How cheap like bargain gas was my motel?

& what goes together quite so well as sirens & a cheap motel?
How cheap was my motel?
A parking lot with pickup trucks
Pickup lines & pizza crusts
A potted artificial palm beside the door
Faded plastic tuffs & full of butts
We could've dated Death herself
For all we wouldn't kiss & tell
How cheap for us was my motel?

It sounded like a car alarm going off
Inside a pervert's skull. Claudia, wake up !
I swoon   I think it's Armageddon
I think it's Friday afternoon   I think it's
Time to sign the pledge   or time to sleep
Inside a boobie's hedge

Only in Lower Chicago
Can someone find the proper sort of cheap motel
How cheap was mine? My cheap motel?
Transfiguration of transient souls
Equipped of course with their internal poles
As they say it's conjoined hip to universal joint
          ENOUGH! ANOINT
THE KEEPER OF THAT SWELL
& THAT'S HOW CHEAP IT WAS
& IT WAS   WAS MY MOTEL

GRANDMOTHER POEM

Myself I couldn't help but
notice growing up where I
did
how all the Polock & Bohunk
kids were afraid
(no... terrified) of their own
            sweet grandmothers called
            Bubbies behind closed doors
Of course there's nothing especially
frail about a pink & gray old lady in
a brown babushka Her fingers are
like the roots of certain oak trees &
she stoops all day in the front yard
yanking up dandelions, cutting
grass with scissors
even though she's 87 (buried her
husband decades ago just folded
him up in a drawer)
& when she' s not yanking up weeds
or raking those same damn
leaves even as they drop
or hosing down the front
sidewalk nine times in a single
week
or washing the glass panes,
or changing screens to
storms or storms back to
screens
or sweeping the snow in the thick of a
blizzard. Then she' s back in her
medieval kitchen warm inside with all
those poppy seeds
& vanilla sugars making all
those endless eastern
European
pastries which although

they taste superb & will not kill,
are nonetheless as foreign as
space rocks heavy enough to
pull a Cossack
down off his horse
(which might have been their original intention)

Her kitchen is still the old country full
of memories, cemeteries & steppe
          tortures of the hideous
          memory: tanks & mass graves
spiked helmets & Ubermenschen,
commissars
& collaborators. No respite,
not even for the Black
Madonna nor the Infant of
Prague atop the Frigidaire
Everywhere the reminder of the slaughter of peasants by hussar or
Tzar
& sepia photos of those same slaughtered
peasants still alive unpronounceable peasant
names   peasant Legs   & peasant lips
 peasant skin thick
As boot leather,
so squat & square no nun
Would be caught dead...
If I had a Bubbie like that   I too Would be afraid growing up
 \here in Chicago with Donald Duck Skippy
Peanut Butter   & Cherry High-C.
Then I too Would want to chop
off pieces
Of my last name   three extra syllables
from The end of myself   ashamed
& proud that the only Slavic words I knew
 were for things like "shut
          up" "go to
                    Mass!" "eat!"
          "..get out of
                    my kitchen"

                   or "wipe
                   Your feet!'
Better not
to have to haul around all that
history   to know too well
whose blood it was, whose peasant
blood fertilized that vast European Plain.

AFTER MASS AT THE BUTCHER'S CASE

Sweet Jesus, but these people
Take their sweet time appraising the almost identical
Cellophane-wrapped slabs of sweet cow. It's the red stuff, Lady,
That's the actual meat, the color of sunset in a Renaissance Crucifixion,
 plus pink Styrofoam,
Enough that it might float.
So there they stand like raptured
Christians as each studies something big in a London Broil...
While a few feet down breasts & thighs
Of disembodied fryers, also cellophaned,
Point upwards towards florescent tubes of Heaven.

Masterworks of Santa Muerta appear in my mind.
Nobody else sees them. Sausage Section melts into Dairy Section
Where deceased cows give way to bottles full
of fermented, cultured milk. Milk & mold, happy as
Wisconsin wet dreams,   bog grass,   marsh hay.
Where is all this mutton...not a hint of wool...coming from?
Lamb-O-God by any other name.

My sacred tongue consists of screaming
Grunting & whispering innuendos in Latin.
When will it all make sense...? Kosher to the left of me
Halal to the right   Soy sausage for recent Buddhists
& face down in the ice among the tilapia,
the lost bandwidth of squandered
Eucharist. So why do I feel so cold at ease?
Why do I feel at all

FART GAS IN THE BIG CITY

Do you love humanity—all of humanity—the sinners blended
in with the saints   the ugly with the beautiful,
your clones
as well as your own doppelgangers   all bound in behind your
eyes?
Or do you love yourself most of all?
Here you are a pedestrian on Michigan
Avenue   like an egg-bound chick across from the Art
Institute. The crowd thickens Sulfur & smog Must be lunch or
quitting time What do you care? `They smell like
everything   like dogs & red roses like vinegar & blood
Can you really love them collectively
like a gigantic thumb up civilization's ass? Or
can you withhold judgment? It's the closeness
the mindless excess of skin   too much breath   one mouth
breathing in what a thousand more expel   What
predator lurks up your nose?
But you like it here east
of the loop   landfill versus the Lake   Air like algae
& dead fish   like Harris Tweed & crematoriums
Smells like your sweetest nightmare all gone to hell
all rising up the subway stairs
Better you should meander here amid the lunch hour
tangle where it's all mini skirts & legs
legs which stretch all the way up into the mind
& Michigan Avenue
which smells like old underwear on a hot day.

DIGGING UP CADAVERS

"Leave the dead to bury the dead"
In a graveyard there are two jobs:
burials & exhumations.

I

You can't go there   not if you don't
Have the proper underwear there & you

Up to your knees in unquiet clay you don't
A mouthful of wine a list in your pocket

Proscribed body parts
The fangs & tattoos & here you thought

A career in journalism might just suit you
Fit the questions into the answers thus

Make a neat cut with the sharp end
Of the short handled spade Good luck

You see there are mausoleums here complete
With false doors better to vent the truth

There are crematoria about with Grecian pillars
Discretely designed to look like libraries

Even the best tomes history & religion
Are filled to overflowing with obvious omissions

Behind every period. A paragraph   or two.
Seems to have been deleted. each comma,

Misdirects in the name of clarity, civil behavior
Leading naked to some preordained conclusion

& is it me or is it me   the ground water seems
To be creeping closer ever closer to the surface

                    II

Observe
White people amusing themselves in black

On the board walk   any boardwalk
Or in the tunnel of love

Casting aspersions
Upon one another   This is living!

Think of Odysseus tied to the main mast
Another busload of tourist sirens

& here you go sorting the recyclables
One foot in the grave already

Egg-sucking weasels referenced already
In THE NATURAL HISTORY OF WEASELS

A BEGINNER'S GUIDE. Harcourt, Brace
Or Maybe Random House one of those

& here you assumed the life of the intellectual
Might just suit you Passionless Sundays

On your knees   Sartre or Spinoza
& that itch that won't go away

                    III

Falling off a mountain   falling off a saddle
Slamming into a façade of bricks

It's apparent that you do not

Play well with others   those damned-ass others

How many times does the yo-yo have to bow
Down to the string? a noose by any other name

Backwhile mean at the ranch
There's the fancy lingerie store right next to

The new tattoo emporium   (Why is it always
Tattoos?)   transparent lace or opaque skin

But it's not a choice a choice is not a choice
Your life is a recurring train wreck

Gravity always owns you in the end
& here you thought the convoluted life

Of a working class philosopher might be
Your best possible fit   Yea

Like there's not enough ignorance in the world
Already   Earthquakes   Volcanoes

& you   you who keeps trying to escape yourself
Like a tortoise trying to escape his own shell

& luck   luck's got nothing to do with it
centrifugal force versus inertia   versus

                    IV

Too many rats & not enough
Rhubarb   It's like licking

A rock & expecting to wake up in granite
(The happy saliva of midnight)

Trailers full of baggage
Small dogs named for phases of the moon

& you you're so tired of this shit
& here you once thought the drum of surrealism

Would help you to dance on the rotating ball room
Otherwise known as Planet Obvious

But what's the hell with all this human skin
The tambour of reality   the itching insistence

That nothing's going to end well
Even the snakes in the snake pit are weeping

& you know all about snakes
Earth wisdom random ad hoc procreation

An ancient goddess who eats her children
Like pills from a bottle

                    V
Eating meat on Good Friday
& there's lots lots more in the fridge

Trying to work your way up through the bubbles
Into the realm of insincere religion

The worship of Gravity
The spiritual quest for Steak& now

There's spinal fluid dripping from something
Resembles a Crucifix

& here you thought a life or reasonable piety
Would be safer like an extra mattress

Like that schizoid priest in the funky closet
Could make it all better with three Hail Marys

& now somebody just let Jesus out of the secure
Holding area   the Green Room

Called Paradise   & here comes Atlantis
Right up on scheduleup from sleep!

& you wake up encased in your c-pap
Mask   with a bladder full of trouble

Full of holes Holes are not halos
Nightmare's not the same as Soul

                    VI

There must be rules to digging/undigging graves
The grid to be respected   always

Rectangles invisible
To the naked eye   Believe

In the absolute hunger
Of all the absolute dirt

To escape the clutch of earth
Volcanoes & erosion

Requires steel cables &
a lazy afternoon

And mud up to your zipper
& to calculate the

Weight of water   eight pounds per
The ratio of cable slack

To the depth of concrete vault
Careful not to let yourself feel

Anything or nothing both being

Approximate causes

Of loop-de-loop madness exhumations
Being more profitable to the boss

In the front office with his plat book
And samples of polished agate

Since somebody wanted a new unbiased autopsy
Or wanted to expand one family's plot

In a shrinking cemetery open
To the public & here you thought

This was a vocation for your own morbid nature
That you the digger in Hamlet were at peace with tragedy

There was dignity in death green grass
& juniper   but be careful indeed

Be especially aware of the living
Who can fill up these open air mausoleums

Like Catholics during lent doing the Stations
Seeking beautified finger bones

                VII

Peeling back on yourself like layers of onion
Memories pungent as old meat

You sit on the three legged stool
At the far edge of the bar your beer

Like a mug of foaming dog piss
Gives you the right to stay here   squatters

Rights suppose somebody recognized you
The deranged sexton   Lord of the Backhoe

Who digs up Jimmy Lee
As a favor (not quite) to the Coroner   that

Busy public servant who decrees cause of death
Was it the tree that killed the Chevrolet?

Or something darker something
In the coffee below the counter served

With malice of forethought pay
Is the same plus reinternment   time

& a half on weekends minus the urgency
Of a Jewish funeral   & here

You thought you were a bit too pure
To measure your life in dollars

                    VIII

Sometimes you'd like to manufacture bombs
From living flesh   to wit

When you can't tolerate all this sadness
When the hemp rope cuts your palm

When the stars can't be kept separate
From the nebulae

When you can't even tolerate righteous indignation
When the acid of angry women permeates the ether

When all the crypto-zoologists deny your own
Existence perhaps to better explain   to dovetail

Strident unforgiving reality
When poems go completely off the rails

When it comes to pass that you and your whole crew
Have to empty a graveyard in order

To expand a highway to relieve the gridlock
Of unexpected townhomes

Which sprouted in real time like mushrooms
Amid the one time flying ears

& here you thought the future was just
A continuation of the past

Interrupted by the present
Staring you yourself in the role of Clark Kent

IX

Bones are for movies   Bones are for deserts
Bones are for dunes & eroded mountains

Bones are for restaurant décor
Think chop sticks & Jolly Rogers painted on black

Think the mummification of Batman
Bones are for Halloween & paper lanterns

Bones are transfigurations of flesh into dust
But not or never here where you grew up

Where bones turn into sludge
Where skeletons are rarer than literal truth

Where the coffin outlasts the body
& the cement vault is almost forever

& the low bidder   remember that
The low bidder's likely to cut some corners

Remove the vaults   but not always
The debris within   for instance when

The vault cracks   something shifts
The whole thing separates kaboom

Then bones are for hiding Bones are for
The airless black clay   Bones are to forget

When you go out for a few oxygenated shots
After the sun goes dark & the digging stops

& here you used to think the absence of irony
Equaled   more of less   the irony of absence

& you the low bidderalways the lowest bidder
Always up to your neck in something

Sometimes it's division by zero
Sometimes it's standing barefoot

In somebody else's grave
Barefoot in somebody else's grave

Hip deep in somebody else's grave
You as naked as a corpse

Wearing someone else's soul
Tied around you like a loin cloth

DRUNK IN LYONS PARK

I am not writing many poems
I am drinking rather too heavily

people worry about me
I am seated in the park beside

a merry-go-round watching
my youngest daughter play

my whole self feels like a pair
of oxen pulling their yokes

in opposite directions
otherwise I'm feeling

no desires   just their absence
like newly missing molars

POEM FOR A MEATLESS FRIDAY

Tonight aunt Mary
& great aunt Ellen both left early
left to go do the stations
at Our Lady of Heavenly Sorrows
for the rest of us
here at the VFW fish fry
it's all you can eat   cash bar downstairs
we contemplate Lenten ashes
get drunk in Lenten conversations
only the very the very silent among us
can hear the belated crowing of a barnyard fowl
three times over

BEHIND THE CURTAIN

Veronica hates Archie
Who is hated by Betty
For whom Jughead represents

An ampersand gone amok
& Richie Rich won't appear
It's all comical bookends

Bad ink in place of color
Archie hates all of Betty
Not just her blonde pony tail

Veronica ain't normal
Red hair with all those hatch lines
That stuff ain't normal either

It's worse than Lois & Clark
Worse than Satan & Milton
Archie wakes up each morning

& vomits up for his lunch
Whatever's going around
In Riverdale High School

Which isn't so much high school
As a concentration camp
Where they put all the white kids

From all North America
Until they never grow up
Or until they switch over

To survivors from
Krypton Beware of green
rocks that glow Or go
back to Riverdale

Which is not river nor dale
It's only America digesting itself
America Digesting America

For whatsoever that's worth
That's all it ever can be
God's mercy upon the rest

BILL RUST DEAD THESE MANY YEARS

Bill Rust dead these many years, now among the
Seraphim but with balls from a dragon's belly, I still Can
see you wrapped like some kind of serpent fresh From
the Garden, wrapped around your father's beige Sofa
back in the decades of hypothetical emergence. Is it me
or is it me, cicadas & bat-winged angels,
How we defied the law of averages by plunging Directly
into the oblivion that goes
By the name of reality! Ducks flying with eagles? Hanging
out on College Avenue with Jesus?
& all that willful ignorance, delivering pizza for beer Money...
Myself, I was just killing time, just time.
For me it wasn't even a game anymore. You'd say,
"Look, there's a raven!"   & I'd go, "No, Bill, it's

Just a crow, just a large crow." Big crows are almost
Never small ravens. & sometimes you'd call a hawk A
phoenix & me, I'd have to remind you, "No, Bill.
That's just a hawk hunting mice in the short grass." No
wonder you got distressed by me sometimes.
Full moons & night-feeding screech
Owls, the Mise-en-scene of those days, I remember it all (Like the glue
remembers the envelope,) but you, You needed no full moon,
just a handful of Valium A fifth of Kirshwasser or the equivalent in E&J
Between the paychecks... ingest & wait... then rocks could
fly.
Then who I loved like another brother, somebody Cain would love
Like another Cain, watching you & you, you would go belly deep into
hell. Your friends walked away.
Your women ran away, including those who once had To
be peeled off you by the application of salt.
You were that much done,
Still living in your father's huge & almost empty frame.
Until that morning we were all told that you woke up On
your father's beige sofa.   Woke up & died.

AT THE INTERSECTION OF SAINT CHARLES

To me she looks way
too young to have such
faded tattoos
inked long before
puberty as for the studs
in her lip all the visible
piercings embedded on
her face those prongs
appear brand new   no
tarnish no matted skin
what does it matter her hair
purple-red with green streaks
 makes for a weird halo?
but she's driving a Camry!
Maybe that's her mommy's car
or her parole officer's car
mid level civil servants drive
such storied chariots
republican bloggers cruise
around like hot green mambas
in similar vehicles
someday there will be earthquakes
to swallow up all our engines
until then we wait it out
like jackrabbits at a red light
myself & this freaky Jungfrau
as we navigate our way
through the coming century

I hate everyone, especially those people I don't like. And I hate the moon. I mean the actual moon. Sunlight hurts my eyes and I always avoid it. My mother never approved of my friends, nor my friends of my mother. I've always hated my friends. Many are the things I do not hate but most of them I do despise. The planet Earth is a grave disappointment to me. The planet Earth is crusted under with graves. Those who insist on having their ashes scattered are polluting our lungs, my lungs, and I hate them for it.

As Chester lay upon the collapsible gurney he saw (even though his eyes were quite shut) a beautiful angel, something as lovely as a sympathy card or a mass card, a perfect seraph, an icon from the 15th century. She (slightly androgynous but definitely a she) floated above him, as if she'd come to take him home. As Chester surged upwards into her arms she suddenly shifted to be standing beside him, almost collapsing the collapsible gurney. Quickly she pulled out a knife and cut him! Cut Chester from his left eyebrow in a circular fashion to his unshaven chin; Chester screamed. The ambulance drive slammed on the brakes. "Hey Chuck! This guy's still alive!" "Yea and he's got blood all over his face. What the fuck's wrong with the triage team?"

Somethings are just impossible to describe. They have no form, or expertise in being extant. A person might not know what the f**k they are if not for hitting their heads against them. And it hurts. Ideas without wombs. Unfinished crossword puzzles. Panhandlers handling pans. Wormwood and marshmallows. Forbidden things with no f**m. Coloratura buglings turning into Chloroptera, Ara. Disappearing mattresses. You w***e up and notice the mi**le of things are going s***h. What to do? Wear a flag for a hat? Tell yours**f, "I'm not getting older. I'm just getting out." Put that in your bag and f**k it. Negativity isn't a bad thing. What serendipitous fool ever decided that? The cereal shot from guns. Going over the falls in a barrel. Going over the falls not in a barrel. A popsicle in the hand melts faster than a stoned woman's heart. So tell me why. Why does sunshine hurt my eyes? Why is malignant melanoma the price the sun bunnies must pay? Where did I leave my taps? I sit in my cloistered space and stare/glare at the jar off alcohol holding the fetal pig. Is the fetal pig also my guardian angel? Myself, I cannot tolerate snickering clowns.

Chester lay in the hammock and pretended to be dead. Ramses the Last, unknown pharaoh of the umpteenth dynasty. It felt great, great to be one with the scarabs. Chester reached for his libation, melted ice and Save-Way scotch. We are civilized people here; we never desecrate cadavers...or corpses either. Chester wondered whatever was the difference. Without using his neck he stared up at the tree with the bat house. Soon the damaged sun would be setting and the bats would emerge. Lepidoptera will converge at the mercury lamps and be eaten. Mosquito abatement trucks will kill them all.

THE GRAVITY MACHINE

Where we keep falling
& falling
until we land in a pile of dirty laundry
& the audience applauds
but the loving cup
& the woman go to the man
With a suitcase for a jaw.
Damn right I'm bitter tonight & I'm beginning to think

This whole steeplechase has been rigged.
Like I'm not involved actively in my own doom,
Like I'm a torn envelope in search of an
Uncancelled stamp, like I have
This expiration date falling after me,
Relentless & filled with something burning.

Where we exchange skins
like rattle snakes schizoid rattle snakes,
then we color ourselves an indifferent gray.

Too bad for the ungrateful lanterns of fate.
My self I'm still capable
of love & tender passion but
I'm not so sure of the secret mouth
screaming in my ear.
who made this world so complicated
that even the bread confuses itself
with the meat?

I'm tired of my
situation, my immense losing streak.
It's the politics of lies & cable news
that make me want
to rename my body.

GOD DESTINY & THE SHOE-BILLED STORK

In your leaky hip waders
perhaps sitting in traffic
discussing theology
with a naked protestant
the next thing the very next thing
a huge flock of those
shoe-billed storks darkens
the entire sky for hours

see you're crawling
between blankets
minding your own personal amore
when a shoe-billed stork passes
thunder lightning & you're toast!

these days I walk with a cane
it makes the absurd easy
I trip over the shoe-billed stork
I regain my balance just in time
not to go splat like an egg
all wrapped up in a diaper
en route to a birthing hospital

FEBRUARY IN A POTEMKIN VILLAGE

Outside it is still snowing
Christmas up from the black weeds
miles off down the road
the Mardi Gras atmosphere
mucks up any agenda
these are cigarettes from hell
breath on frigid afternoons
outside it is so empty
no birds at the bird feeder
no dog walkers walking dogs
& no stray pedestrians
to occupy the sidewalk
like Robinson Crusoe
upon a melting glacier
I watch out for rising oceans
outside there are no oceans
outside there is only snow
which threatens to turn to rain
if I had a good cigar
then I wouldn't be afraid
to start playing with fire
instead I'm rubbing my palms
left hand against the right hand
friction instead of anger
outside I have no idea
it's just the Fahrenheit
or deeper isolation
that puts me into this mood
except this mood keeps following
like a spaniel at my heel
my extremities stay numb
for hours   no smoke rises
I stretch out on the sofa
& listen to the faucets drip

I FELL ASLEEP AT THE POETRY READING

...just couldn't tolerate the exquisite
smallness of things
as if each word was an alpine flower
crusted to alpine mud
like the Thorne miniatures only smaller
or like Colleen Moore's cutaway dollhouse
or like a Thomas Kinkade Potemkin
calendar shrunk down to fit
on a debit card   like guppies-sized fish
stuck at the bottom of the tank
meanwhile outside ambulances screamed
not at poetry but at Toyotas
which wouldn't get the hell
out of their way cretins in center lanes
who would not yield no Dante
to give warning   no grim reaper
to remind them of the laws of physics
        & the angel of death
then I woke up woke too abruptly
me my wife my chief confessor
& a roomful of MFAs from Evanston
poetry reading over
I had to crawl out from under the carnage
like Francis Villon looking
for his machine gun   his machine gun
& a clean pair of pants

THESE ARE POEMS THAT DON'T WRITE THEMSELVES

I

These are poems that don't write themselves
These are pieces of your birthing sarcophagus

They drip like coagulated news from the 24 hour news crews
A twig snaps   Somebody screams   fade to jugular black

We've been here before   in lifeboats   in
rubber rafts Waste-deep in the sludge of argument
                           the pacifists Among
us bleeding profusely from paper cuts...

Is it a nightmare to want to kiss your mother's corpse?
To shake your fist at those who taught you to dance?

Is it a serious sin to regret nothing?
To go on fucking the air & saying out loud repeating often
That no bad thing has ever happened   no real thing
happened

A bone breaks   this was unintentional
We were just horsing around   playing at war

THE ROSES OF EXPERIENCE

with a bladder-full of champagne I am
about to water the roses   let's see
on the one hand you've got the roses
of experience   later there are
the roses of unintended consequence
you've got your red roses & your brown roses

& someday I am going to water them all

 & someday after they have my taps bronzed
 I'm going to jitterbug barefoot amid

the absolute decay of roses

 yellow fumes from dead skin so that when
 them bones actually do rise again

I'm there to play the wicked tambourine

SURVIVOR'S LOGBOOK

I

This here's my heart
exactly the size of my fist
& these are my lungs
about the same as two
lunch bags full of the air
we all exhale
        into the poisoned dawn
my brain is the purple
& red/gray melon
you would not want
        to sleep in the same bed
where I sleep not
knowing what harm
it could do if it exploded
& these are my testicles
        what's left of them
after the emergency erection
that almost killed me

II

when I woke next morning
the cat lady was gone
so were all 14 of her cats
plus her black turtleneck
her floor length black coat
her black leather mini skirt
her black satin underwear
        not to mention her black
make-up bag full
of black lipstick
black eye-shadow green
mascara & what looked
like demented rosary beads
& anyhow the sky

        though queasy was clear
& the tractor I rode in on
was splayed upon its back
with its treads still smoking
as dead as a steer
in Wyoming

        III

between these sheets I slept
as if through an earthquake
& this mattress only looks
like the edges of the Grand Canyon
roll off & you're underwater
where there are mermaids
all of them starved for the flesh
of drowned sailors
of which I am not!

WHILE PLANTING PURPLE PETUNIAS IN VILLA PARK

Women shaped like green bottles
confuse my best intentions

My life has grown too complicated
like a game of 3-D chess

it's time to dig a new Eden
from these fine steel implements

I will create my herbage thus;
bulbs will sprout up everywhere

things will rectify themselves
the garden gnome will be me

POP GOES THE WEASEL

I'm not an idiot but I act like one
especially when the seasons are
off alignment & my belly screams
like the unknown primate   or when
the posse forgets that
I'm supposed to be the sheriff
it's already half of May
& already the umbrellas are all AWOL
my test scores are quite high
they tell me & I ought to be off
in the clouds somewhere
directing zeppelins   but I feel
like an idiot stranded here on earth
surrounded by puddles of rancid milk
my idiot bone & my idiot gland
have never been larger
but I am no idiot   all this
malarkey not withstanding
just idiot-spawn perhaps
but not the thing itself

STILL LIFE IN A TRAGIC YEAR

A man sits at his desk trying
to look important
too many wars going on
the man looks like a vacant
space   too many exit
wounds in his brains   not enough
gauze & plasma
so he just sits there almost
nodding like water
in gentle wind
see! There in no turmoil in his heart
just a plastic breath
just as a plastic stone breathes
in-out out-in
slowly like a broken metronome
& one room over a blue macaw
speaks in the secret language of parrots

PARTS OF MY BODY POEM (#17 THE APPENDIX)

which in my case I haven't got
got cut out in '55 by some long dead
surgeon from back when a cutter
cut most everything tumors to taxes
I thought they were trying to kill me
the ether   the mask   the defunct hospital
but what was trying to kill me my own
vestigial self   the scar remaining for half
a century now anchored deep in my belly
but sometimes when perhaps the moon
is leaking through the brown glass bottle
I can't help wondering how many vestigial
parts still fester within   organs   organelles
& tissues they don't have names for
calcified gargoyle heads embedded
in the liver   extra calcified brains
remnants of the third eye   blind
as any thumb but I go thinking myself wet
like any drunken slob
with Germans for ancestors Irish men
who slept with German women who
begot my entire line
I think about all of them & wonder
what other parts have already
been removed without
my knowledge or consent
I think about my father's small ghost
a man who lived with unkind
premonitions of death   my father never returned
My appendix never grew back either
when that reaper cut out my daddy he
cut me so deep I've yet to recover
still limp I do like a professional bull rider

STILL LIFE WITHOUT PUMPKINS

Here there is only white noise
from the air filter
in the tropical tank
platys & tetras swimming
all the rest of their exothermic lives
all in the same dreary 10 gallons
plus the hiss of black
stale tobacco such as a Russian
peasant might ignite
after vodka & tea   plus
the hum of a dying Fridgidaire
enough to make you fear
for bacteria growing in the slaw

soon the mice will attempt
to migrate indoors
nesting in my stucco walls
eavesdropping on
my winter conversation

so too will my multiple personas
attempt migration
to the same vodka-infested jungles
of a wicked human heart
it's like a Joseph Conrad novel
poured over wilted lettuce

LOST OUTSIDE THE WOMB

I

So how come you're all still so new at this,
breathing in vast lungs-full of hypothetical
cold fire, not even able to curse your fate?
You sit & rot here listening to the BBC
          while the world keeps   turning.

II

(What time is it?)
There's nothing much to drink in here
but badly bruised bad whiskey.
& how come nobody
                    living here is welcome
sharing your mattress?
                              Nor able
to explain the movement of stars over
the drunken millennia?   Except to say
the entire Universe is pulling
herself apart like a newly enraptured jellyfish.

III

& you have forgotten the exact shape
of a jelly (an umbrella with tentacles),
which you used to know quite well
the way the arrow used to know the bow,
the way the marrow used to know the bone.
Things used to belong all tucked up inside of here,
vacant gardens of huge melody,
Django Reinhardt playing the stoned blues
against infinity...

IV

& then we all get born.

LAST POET IN AMERICA

I am the last poet
waiting out here for free
bread & fish
I am also your last flag wanting to be
pulled down after taps
I am your last falling star
your last speckled angel
I've survived all the unmarked
intersections & abandoned parking
I've outlived all the groovers/psycho movers
those written as if by god's fingers
on all the beaches of this uncertain earth
between the low tides of May
& the ripe tsunamis of July here I am
still going like a '57 Chevy whereas
all my friends with names like Bill
or Chuck are filling up urns
victims of cool stupidity or relentless
gravity off somewhere in some
insane Paradisio composed mostly
of traffic cones & cigarettes
they didn't make it & croaked but me
I didn't make it either & remained
& occasionally I hear rumors
of one who's pouring sidewalks
in California or the one who left for
Indiana or the one who hung up
his Les Paul in favor of cryogenics
I tell you there's a thread attached
to each cadaver's toe
except my own
myself here I stand still waiting for fish
& bread the last poet of my race
& I know everything about myself
except my true name   feeling more
like the bones of the umbrella
than the umbrella itself

INTERSECTIONS

I stand naked without an umbrella
in a raw puddle among such people
who will not share their own umbrellas

can't tell a street from an avenue anymore
but wait beside the red for the signal
to change breathing in fumes but the signal
refuses to flicker going green not at all

back in Texas my wife dresses in black silk
either for cocktails or a funeral
which one she will not tell but only that
she'll be back way after midnight
& not to wait up by the stovepipe

meanwhile this guy on crutches
who looks more like me than I do
he rushes out in front his pants
are filled with spider webs his manner
of hustle it reminds me
of a planet in full eclipse where am I?

TIMES OF SUFFOCATION

Still only morning & the sun
has barely cleared
Bob Stezowski's ancient arborvitae
the tallest cypress
this side of Salt Creek
is that a garage sale or an eviction?
So many people losing their homes!
These are times of suffocation
excuse me if I cross over
to the west side of the avenue
tongues wag without real fire
I feel as though I'm priced to sell
I feel like good real estate gone bad
I shuffle on like a judge   a hanging judge
looking for his black robe   hanging
perhaps from a thorn-bearing crab
shrike meat   economic meltdown
false gods die falsely then
the false god named optimism
(renamed Moloch) named freedom
as in the freedom to suckle
at the teats of a dead sow
milk & urine business & handshakes
I keep walking this suburban blight
past piles of abandoned sofas

TWO TENTS

A north-fork pine on a wide window's ledge
nowadays used as a bookend, it still
reminds me of northern Arizona in springtime
outside Jerome--
the ceder forest I almost wandered off in--
Catching me beyond the campfire,
she led me back, all the way back
to my own tent, she to hers, two tents
two different tents
& a gulf of so many years.

WINFIELD ILLINOIS
meditation upon my mother's 100th birthday

My people are all buried
up to their necks
in adjective envy
in memories   & worse
those empty regions
where there are no ghosts
or fugues   just large cemeteries
with smaller graveyards all locked
up inside
here the graveyards outnumber
the actual dead   dead selves
bones & pieces of souls
or spirit   or shadow   or flickers
expanding like a dust storm
my people are obsessed with dust
with their own rituals nouns tripping
over prepositions   grief
& the inability to mourn
a grave   a bed   a scaffold
perhaps a podium   a paper airplane
my people know how a single folded
sheet can so upend the laws of nature
gravity itself   migration   amnesia

THE PURGATORY TREE

Out this window looking over
   the suburb primeval
   I watch how the leaves are falling
    without really turning
     Walking in backyard (unstable ground)
      right cane (support) lift   step
     left cane (balance) lift   step
    repeat lift   step   lift   step
   Keeping eyes on the lawn
always down where tripping
is not allowed
  doesn't shape into falling
   & bones don't break
   At last I get my whole self
    over to Grandfather Sycamore
   Which has become a separate part of me
  I have named my Purgatory Tree
This time is dark   Never have
I known a darker time (lift step)
Each night getting longer
 The parchment crunch
  of withered leaves
   in mummified repose
   the comatose response
   of black sugar dirt
  It's too tired to snicker
Too difficult to pray
This tree this Grandfather Sycamore
embalmed in its own life's sap
 shedding bark as easily as summer's leaves
  This tree was here before we came
   before the white man with his plows
   of iron   This tree older
   than the last genocide
  not the Tree Of the Knowledge
 Of Good and Evil
nor the World Ash

Not the sacred oaks of my ancestors
  Not the Tree of absolute Gehenna
    This is no forest. Do you see a forest here?
     Can you hear the saber rattle of dying ash?
      But carbon fumes & sirens will tell you
       the damn highway   mother of asphalt fumes
   The highway has no horizon
 & the numbness of you telling
your own face to ignore itself
talk about trees
  talk about the Ceders of Lebanon
  talk about that mad prophet
Amos   a dresser of sycamores
  talk a bout all the jackpine recently burnt
    due perhaps to lightning & drought
      or talk about The Tree of Life
   which takes away the sting of passing
   the parasite tree
the paradise tree
  the tree which feeds off the oasis
    but myself I'm at a loss for trees
      out of rational trees & never known
       a darker time   time of shedding bark
     time of suicidal leaves
   Me & Grandfather sycamore
   together on uneven ground unable to decide
do we ignore all this suffering
or embrace all this suffering
  Plagues winds floods fires freaks
   of the natural orders
     my country fermented inside
      its own hatred   of its own self
        of all its component parts
     Then let this be my Purgatory tree
     my tree of atonement
  sap & blood for a tragic time
right cane lift   step   left
cane lift   follow

IDIOM OF THE AMERICAN BOY

Sooner or later they shall be compelled to know me as their own
native son of a native son
born on the same mutant tangle
they call their Heartland
ungrateful SOB seven generations
removed from Thomas Jefferson's
failed utopia.

Come that day they will have no choice
but to acknowledge me
the same meat
as the Pilgrims' meat,
same pale pink epidermis that
makes them all so damned pure and whole,
Latex Teflon skin--
     Polyester and DEVOURER.
Oh, yes they will.
They will know me by the flatness
of my unaccented English
& the hardness of my religion,
my solid brass Cadillac Jesus heart,
    by which they shall know me.

They will learn that I am not
their blue-eyed boy back here for nothing,   no, no
returning supplicant come to make peace, or to be reconciled,
or to keep the faith, any damn faith, or to keep
a promise made under duress, or to salute the National Cadaver,

      not me
not to go sticking my fingers up
   their lowest corporate demographic or
     to applaud when nothing's wonderful.

But still... they will still see me there at the Fairgrounds
in that Biblical hamlet, called Wheaton, Illinois,
eating rattlesnake candy, leaning up there against the rails

at the demo derby   cheering the redneck Chevy
each time she broadsides the white-bread Ford...

& they will watch me leering at their daughters,
Lot's daughters, the same daughters,
        daughters of Eve's daughters, their navel rings glinting in the
                                                                arcade-lit
                night as they lick
their cones, their red frozen sugar cherry painted mouth parts,
                        Making like moths at forbidden orbs.
& they will feign at shock & alarm...

        but I am just
        the monster they made themselves by being merciful.
I've passed through them like nitrous oxide, like obnoxious allies,
like tainted underwear.
That was me on backups singing
"Hey Joe where are you going with that gun in your hand?"

& they will know who I am.   Oh yes they will.
They've seen my type before   & sure
they will try to render me statistically insignificant.

& they will point to their graveyards full of iron poles and plastic flags
& barely remember their Union Dead & they will set off
their 4th of July explosions from a safe distance, whole families of
them on picnic shrouds & the air so thick with DEET
& adolescent pants   that there's no room left to exhale.

& they will shrug and say sure we have a few
bad apples   bad bad apples
                        meaning me
but they will know me
        & they will know me by all my other names
        & know me as well by my angry shoes & missing teeth
                & know me as well by this sign, call it the mark of Cain,
                        as if tattooed upon my hungry skull.

73

Rick Duffey was born near Chicago halfway through the 20th century. He has worked as a mail carrier, a landscaper, a gravedigger and gravestone setter, a machinist, a truck driver, an egg roll maker, a bookseller and substitute teacher. He writes poems because he has to. There is no other excuse.